The Art Of Designing And Manufacturing Woollen Cloth: With Tables, Giving The Dents In Reed, Runs, Twists, Yards, Ounces, Picks, Number Of Threads, Etc. ......

W. C. Barnard

WOOLLEN MANUFACTURES.

THE

ART OF DESIGNING

AND

MANUFACTURING

WOOLLEN CLOTH:

WITH TABLES,

GIVING

THE DENTS IN REED, RUNS, TWISTS, YARDS, OUNCES,
PICKS, NUMBER OF THREADS, ETC.; FINISHING
DEPARTMENT, GIGGING-ROOM, AND
FULLING-ROOM.

———

BY W. C. BARNARD,

CAVENDISH, VERMONT.

———

BOSTON:
A. WILLIAMS & CO.,
100, WASHINGTON STREET,
1869.

PRATT BROTHERS,

Stereotypers and Printers,

37 CORNHILL, BOSTON.

PREFACE.

— ⧓ —

IN giving this work to the public, I do not deem it necessary to preface any excuse. I tender my thanks to LUCIAN WALCOTT, Superintendent of the Elmville Mills, Rhode Island; DWIGHT SUMNER, Agent of the Newark Woollen Mills, New Jersey; DAVID ALGER, Overseer of the Carding Department, Burrillville, Rhode Island; and others, for many kind and valuable suggestions.

I am, yours truly,

W. C. BARNARD.

CAVENDISH, VERMONT. }
Dec. 6th, 1868. }

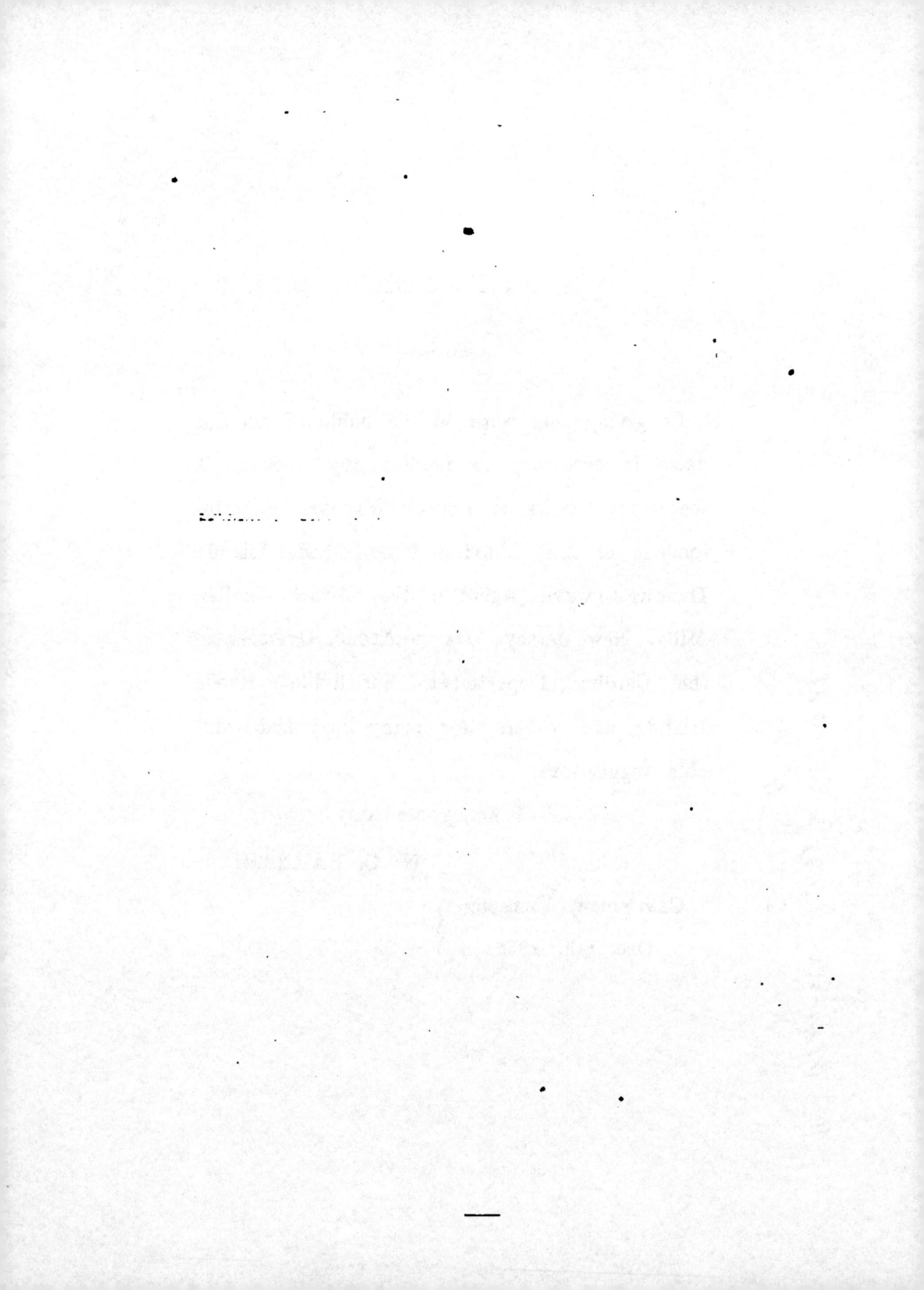

CONTENTS.

———⋈———

CONTENTS.

WOOLLEN MANUFACTURES.

GENERAL OBSERVATION ON WOOL.

WOOL is the filamentous substance which covers the skins of sheep, and some other animals, as the beaver, the ostrich, the llama, the goats of Thibet, of Cachemir, etc. These varieties of wool serve for the manufacture of various styles of fabric, used for raiment and other purposes, under the name of doeskin, cassimere, broadcloth, beavers, flannels, etc. Sheeps' wool alone possesses the fulling or felting property. Wools have been distinguished in commerce into two classes, — fleece wool and dead wool. The first is obtained from the annual shearing of sheep; the last is that cut or pulled from dead animals, and are characterized by their harshness, weakness, and incapacity of taking a good dye, especially if the animal has perished from a malignant disease.

Sheeps' wool is greatly modified by the breeding of the animals, for it is a coarse, hairy substance, mixed with a soft down close to the skin on the wild moufflon; to which genus all the varieties of the domestic sheep have been traced. The merino sheep was first introduced into this country by Consul Jarvis, of Springfield, Vermont. Their fame for fine wool was soon acknowledged to be preeminent. By crossing and mixing with the native blood, they soon produce a fine, strong, healthy fibre, much sought after by the manufacturer for goods of light weight.

It has been ascertained that the female has more influence than the male, on the bodily form of an animal; but that the male, in sheep particularly, gives the peculiar character to the fleece. The produce of a breed from a coarse-wooled ewe and a fine-wooled ram will give a fleece approaching half-way to that of the male; and a breed from the progeny, with a fine-wooled ram will yield a fleece differing only one-fourth from that of the sire. By producing in the opposite ratio, the wool

would degenerate into its primitive coarse-
ness. The hardness of some of the American wools does not depend entirely on the
race or the climate, but on certain pecu-
liarities in the soil, which affect the pas-
ture. The fleece of sheep fed on chalky
districts is generally harsh; that of those
fed on light, rich, high, and dry lands,
like those of Windsor County, Vermont,
are distinguished for their silky softness,
and ready adaptation for its fulling qualities.

The felting property of wool is in some
manner proportional to the softness, and
depends conjointly on the annular, and
other regosities of the filaments observable
by means of a good microscope, and on
their elasticity. In consequence of this
structure, when they are pressed and rolled
together they become convoluted and en-
tangled by mutual friction.

The grease or yolk of the fleece is a
species of soap secreted by the sheep, and
consists of oil, with a little potash. Hence
it serves to facilitate the scouring of wool
by means of water alone, with which it

forms a kind of suds, or emulsion. It is most abundant in those breeds which grow the softest fleeces, and on the part of the back covered with the finest wool. This yolk, however, though favorable to the growing fleece, becomes injurious to it after it is shorn, and ought to be immediately removed, otherwise it will produce fermentation in the wool-heap, and render it hard and brittle, — a change which takes place most rapidly in hot weather. Sometimes the fleece is washed with cold water, on the animals, before shearing; but when it is thick, as in the merino breed, it is washed after it is shorn, either with cold or hot water, the latter being most effectual.

Wool loses in the process from thirty to fifty per cent of its weight. In the last few years, the growers of wool, stimulated by the high prices, have given their atten-tion to producing weight of fleece, and lost sight of quality, which has had a tendency to drive the manufacturer from the home market, to seek his stock where less imposition is practised.

The American wool has altered for the worse. Mr. Woodward, of Woodstock, Vermont, speaking of stock used in his mill, says, that he could not make the class of goods called for by his customers, without mixing Australian, Smyrna, and Mestizo wool, which, being short, fine, and silky, easily takes a high polish and lustre in finishing.

WOOL–SORTING

Is doubtless one of the most difficult branches of woollen manufacturing. It requires a person of long experience, and sound, steady judgment, to value by the fineness, soundness, softness, density, uniformity, and whiteness of its fibres. There can be no rule to work by. The qualities have to be estimated as accurate as the judgment will allow by the manufacturer, wool-sorter, and wool-dealer. When properly prepared, it is handed over to the

WOOL–SCOURER;

Who has a kettle, holding about one hundred and fifty gallons, which is convenient for scouring from twenty to twenty-five pounds of wool at a time.

To commence with a fresh scour, you have to fill the kettle two-thirds with water, and the other third with stale urine. Raise the temperature to one hundred and forty degrees Fahrenheit; enter the above quantity of wool; work it well with the stick, so as to have every fibre exposed to the action of the liquor; and, after about ten minutes' immersion, heave it on the scray, to drain. Then enter another similar quantity; and proceed as before. Take this out, and enter a third quantity. Heave out, and drain this a short time; then throw it into the wash-box, and commence rinsing. The two former kettlesful now return into the liquor again, so that the one which was steeped the first may go into the kettle after the other two. The reason for thus returning the two first scourings into the kettle again before rinsing, is because the same liquor is not in a fit state to dissolve, or render soluble, the fatty substance adhering to the wool until after the third or fourth scour. If it be properly cleaned, it will exhibit the following characteristics : — It will drain quickly, and, as the water leaves it, begins to spring and swell gently up. It will look bright and white, and have a glistening appearance when seen by transmitted light; or, taking it up in the hand, it feels light and lofty. On shaking it over, it readily parts asunder, falling lightly and feather-like. It leaves no stickiness upon the hand; and it smells sweet, having no scent of the sheep or grease about it. On the contrary, if the wool be badly scoured, or set in the grease while it is yet in the wash-box, it will cling together more heavily, and feel weighty on the stick. On throwing it out, it dries slowly; it clings together and cannot be separated; it is clammy, and greases the hand; it is yellow, and dirty-looking; and the most casual observer will perceive that there has been some improper management of it. It will have to be re-scoured.

If, by any accident, you should happen to have a scour of this description, the best plan you can take with it is to make a solution of soap in clean water, at one hundred and seventy degrees, and pour in a little olive-oil; work it in this five or ten minutes, then wash out. You will do well now to look to your scour-kettle, to prevent a like recurrence. As the scour-liquor by use gets thicker, and acquires more consistence, it will start the grease quicker and better; and, by the second or third day after setting, will be in as good condition as it ever will be. One care, therefore, ought to be, to pre-serve it in this solution all the time. In order to secure this object, every morning, before commencing work, take care to skim off all the thick scum that rises on the top during its repose through the night, and scoop out from the bottom all the sand and earthy matter that settle there, — the wool always containing more or less of it. If, after the scour has been set some time, it should get unnecessarily thick, heave out some of the liquor, and replenish with water, and rather more urine than usual. It will scour better after this reno-vation than before. I would observe here that we should so adjust the body of the scour as to be thick enough to start the grease easily, and yet not leave it so thick as to require an unnecessary quantity of water to carry off all the suds. This state is best represented on the second or third day after it is set.

It is a practice among dyers not to be so particular in scouring wool for kettle-colors as for blue-dyeing. This arises from false ideas, and I see no reason whatever for such a distinction. On the contrary, I press it forcibly upon the attention of both manufacturers and dyers, that for all colors, the wool can never be too clean. I will illustrate this a little.

Suppose the grease not to have been sufficiently started in the scour. In this case, water will not have any effect to force the grease from the wool; and you will find that it handles greasy and sticky to the fingers. We proceed to dye it of some common color, — say black, olive, drab, etc. It. is true that the color will appear tolerably well; but let us follow it through the process of manufacturing, and trace out

the final results. In the first place, this
wool will be found to card badly, and require more than clean wool, in order to
overcome the resistance exhibited by the
adhesiveness of the greasy paste left upon
it previous to coloring. It makes, also,
considerable more dirt and waste than ordi-
narily, which becomes a serious loss, if
long continued. It spins badly, breaking,
and not drawing-out, or making as fine,
even, or strong yarn as it otherwise would
do. It does not weave so well either.
But it is in the subsequent operations of
scouring and finishing that we are to look
for its worst effects, for the flannels can
scarcely ever be scoured clean; and if they
should be, it is only to be done by re-
peated scouring and dyeing, or by the em-
ployment of a scour-liquor of such excessive
alkaline strength as not only to injure the
texture and fulling property of the cloth,
but almost to destroy the color, which will
look dull, lifeless, and poor. The cloth
itself will have a dead, lustreless appearance,
and it is utterly impossible ever to get that
high steam polish upon the goods, which

constitute the chief excellence and beauty of modern improvements in finishing. The consequence is, such goods go to market and sustain a loss proportionate to the above defects in their manufacture. Like results follow, when, after fairly starting the grease, we neglect to wash out all the suds; for, in the process of dyeing, the metallic, or earthy salts, such as sulphate of iron, sulphate of copper, alum, etc., enter into combination with the soapy matter left in the wool. The suds of such salts, uniting with the alkali of that soap and the metallic, or earthy base, combining with the grease, forms, by this double decomposition, a mineral soap, perfectly insoluble, and which can never be separated from the fabric by any other process whatever. This will suffice to show the absolute necessity of having the wool properly cleaned, even for the most common shades; and the dyer will perceive how essential it is to his interest to have a perfectly clear ground on which to place his colors; for, on clean wool, the colors take easily, look bright, and are permanently fixed; and every subsequent process of manufacturing has a tendency to improve the beauty and lustre of the colors and the fabric.

I may appear to have been rather prolix on this subject, but I think I have said no more than its importance requires; and I again repeat, it will do as well for us to see, in commencing this preparatory step to dyeing, be certain to begin right, making a clear foundation, and leaving nothing that can afford resistance to the free action of the dyestuffs upon the wool; for, upon the mutual and intimate combination of these, depend the beauty and preeminence of our colors.

Mr. Winslow, of Woodstock, Vermont, a dyer of many years' experience, speaking of preparations for scouring wool and woollens, says that urine is the only natural scour. It leaves the fibre sound, and should be used in preference to anything else.

OBSERVATIONS ON DYEING WOOL.

After scouring the wool, let it remain and drain until the next day. Then take it to the kettle; shake it out, breaking the flakes, and lightening up the whole pile, opening it thoroughly, taking out all the twisted and hard lumps, which, if left in, would take an uneven color. When you have shaken it thoroughly, run up the kettle with water to a proper working height. This will check the boiling, and you can enter the wool more easily, and it will give it a better chance of coloring in an even manner. Then take out the bugs, always bearing in mind to rake up the kettle well before entering the wool. You will now enter the wool as quickly as possible, using the poles until you perceive the color to have taken on every portion of it alike, then press the whole under the liquor. This operation lasts from fifteen to thirty minutes, according to the size of the kettle and quantity of wool to be dyed. Get on a boil as quick as possible; and

2*

continue this at a brisk and steady rate for two hours, with an occasional putting in a lever to aid the boil in changing the position of the wool, if that be required. This time being expired, you will prepare to sadden by running the kettle up with water, and stopping the boil. Then heave in the levers, and, while the men are working this as before, throw on your mordant, or sadden in such a manner, that, by the time the whole of this is ended, the wool may be evenly imbued with it. This takes up about as much time as the first breaking-up. Now press the whole under the liquor, and get on a stiff boil, which continue at a brisk and steady rate for one hour. Then draw off your fire, or steam; run the kettle to the brim with water, and let all remain in during the night, excepting such cases as are expressly specified to the contrary in the recipe for producing them. For preparation colors, once using the lever is sufficient, with two hours' boiling; and, for finishing the same off in a fresh liquor, once handling over, and one hour's boiling, is all that is necessary. For such colors as are dyed off at one operation, a good use of the lever on commencing, and occasional turn of the wool in the kettle, with one hour's boil, is all that is required to complete them.

There are but three general methods, or processes, of dyeing wool or woollen goods, or, in other words, distinct plans of combining colors in a chemical manner with animal fibres. I shall attempt to give an account of them, with an explanation of the theory upon which these combinations take place. The first that I shall describe is that process wherein all the materials that enter into the composition of the color are mingled together in one common liquor, or bath, and applied to the wool at once, by about one, or one and a half hour's boiling. If, into a clear solution of log wood, fustic, or other kind of dyestuff, you pour another solution of any metallic or earthy salt, or sulphate of iron, alum, etc., you will observe, when this mixture takes place, the liquor becomes broken, and a flocky or curd-like matter is formed, which gradually settles to the bottom of the vessel in which the mixture was made. This precipitate is the color which, in this first mode of dyeing, — for we really and positively see the union take place between the coloring principle and the earthy or metallic salt, — the combination of which two substances forms or makes the color we intend to apply to the wool. It also explains the true theory of the formation and constitution of colors; showing them to be a chemical compound, the elements of whose composition are an undefined coloring principle, distributed abundantly through the vegetable and mineral kingdom, and an earthy substance, or a metallic oxide. Although this flocky substance, which is the new-formed color, gradually subsides to the bottom, and leaves the liquor but slightly tinged, yet it is not an insoluble precipitate, but is partially soluble in water, and more particularly at a boiling heat; and on this slight degree of solubility hangs the property it possesses of forming a chemical union with the wool. Did it form an insoluble precipitate, no chemical combination could take place by this mode of dyeing;

because the wool, or cloth, being boiled in a liquor containing nothing but an insoluble powder, no chemical action could take place between them, and the wool would be merely stained, and this insoluble precipitate only adhering to it, and that with but a slight mechanical force. The simple operation of washing in water would be sufficient to remove it.

As said before, this partial solubility of the color is the cause of its union with the wool; for, on immersing the latter in the liquor, it immediately seizes the part held in the solution (the affinity between the color and the wool being greater than between the water and the color). The water, thus robbed of what it held in solution, now dissolves another portion of the color, which is again taken up by the wool; and so on, portion after portion, until the whole becomes fairly combined with the wool, having all been dissolved successively by the water before it could enter into a close and intimate combination with the animal fibre. This mode of dyeing requires a rapid ebullition during the time of coloring, as the greater the heat and agitation given to the water, the more· finely are the broad, flocky particles broken and cut up; and, in proportion to the minuteness of the coloring molecules, so will be the intensity of the shade.

Although this method of dyeing be more expeditious than either of the other two, yet I do not consider it equal to them, either in brilliancy or permanency of color. This plan is more generally used for coloring yarn, flannels, and cloth, especially the finer colors; but you will find it resorted to in several of the recipes in wool-dyeing.

The second mode of applying the color is known by the dyers by the appropriate terms of "Preparing," and its operations are performed in this manner:—After the dye-stuffs have been sufficiently boiled to extract all their coloring matter, the wool is entered, and two or two and a half hours' boiling given to it. This is the preparing part of the process, and the wool only receives in it the slight tinge of color peculiar to an extract of the dyestuffs used in making the liquor. Longer boiling than the above time is needless, as all the color necessary to produce the best effect is in that time combined in the wool.

The next stage is the saddening, or giving it to the mordant, which consists of some chemical salt, such as sulphate of iron, sulphate of copper, alum, etc. The manner of doing which is laid down in the article "On the Operations of Dyeing." In the first of this process, a combination is effected between the wool and the coloring matter, analagous to that which takes place between the astringent, or tannin principle; and the rawhide is the process of tanning. Let us illustrate this a little:—

Make a decoction of any of the dye-stuffs,—logwood, or fustic, for instance; then. pour into this decoction a weak solution of gelatine, and you will perceive that a precipitate falls of the color of the solution of the dyestuffs employed, and a great quantity of color has been abstracted from the decoction. This precipitate is the glue and the coloring matter, which, by their mutual affinities, have formed a compound

that is insoluble in water. Of a similar
nature is the union resulting from the
boiling of wool in the solution of most of
the dyestuffs. In the saddening part of the
process, both the coloring matter and the
wool have a strong affinity for the metallic
or earthy salts. These are drawn by them
in an increased attraction, and a trifle compound of animal matter, the coloring principle and the mineral base of color is formed,
which being held together by virtue of
the three separate forces, offers such a resistance, that boiling water cannot disunite
them. Precisely similar are all the unions
of coloring matter with wool, no matter
what process may have been employed to
effect it.

PREPARATION AND FINISHING.

This is exactly the reverse of the second
mode, and consists of two distinct stages;
in the first of which, the wool is boiled
for two or two and a half hours, and
suffered to remain all night in a solution
of the metallic or earthy salts, that form

the mordant or base of the color you wish to produce. They have a strong tendency to unite with the wool, inasmuch that, on coming out of the preparation, it is in general tinged with the shade peculiar to the oxide of the metal used; and so tenacious is its power of adhesion, that after the coloring matter originally used shall have faded off, or undergone a material change, the property of the mordant remains unaltered, for it will absorb fresh coloring matter as readily as before. After coming out of the preparation, it is customary to wash the wool.

In the second part of this process, a bath of clean water is prepared, in which the dyestuffs are boiled till all the color be extracted. In this, the mordanted wool is dyed up, occupying one or one half hour's time in boiling. In this case, the wool and the mordant both have an affinity for the coloring matter. Their joint forces attract it from the water with such impetuosity, that it is immediately and rapidly united with them, and the color is soon brought out. For this reason, the finishing part of the process requires expert workmanship in order to have the wool evenly dyed. The same colors, dyed by this process, are more superb and permanent than by either of the other plans; but the method requires more time and labor, and is also more expensive than either of the other modes.

ON THE HEIGHTENING OF COLORS.

This operation cannot be considered a distinct process, but only a continuation or additional part of any of the above processes, and is generally performed either in a clean liquor, or a portion of the dyeing-bath is run off, and fresh water added to the remainder, to bring it to the proper temperature. The articles used for this purpose, or as alterants to the shade, are commonly either alkalies or acids. The raising of pinks and crimsons, and the raising of Prussian blue by alkalies, and the heightening and stripping of cloth-dyed blacks (that are rusty and foxy) by acids, are a few examples of colors requiring this extra operation to produce the shade sought for. The temperature in these cases is about one hundred and twenty-five degrees. From these observations, it will appear plain that there can only be three plans of combining colors with wool : —

First, — By applying the whole color at one operation. .

Second, — By combining the coloring matter with the wool, and then giving it the mordant.

Third, — In fixing the mordant on the wool first, and then applying the coloring-matter afterwards.

In giving these recipes, I wish it distinctly understood that they are perfectly reliable. These same directions have given color to goods that have commanded the highest market price ; in fact, have governed the American market for the past ten years, and will continue to be relied upon as the standard of colors, as long as sheeps' wool is converted into clothing, and worn by the human race. In dyeing these colors, great care should be taken to have everything clean in the dye-house, and about the kettle. It is also necessary to clear the water previous to making the dyeing liquors; and this is done by throwing into it a pound or two of alum and three or four quarts of wheat bran, and after letting it lay in awhile, skim off the bran before the water comes to boil. This carries out all the impurities of it, purges or purifies the water as above at all times for all the fine and delicate colors. These recipes are designed for one hundred pounds of wool, if not otherwise ordered.

FUSTIC YELLOW.

PREPARATION PROCESS.

Potash-sulphate of alumina, 10 lbs.
Supertartrate of potash, $2\frac{1}{2}$ lbs.
Murio-sulphate of tin, $2\frac{1}{2}$ lbs.
Boil two hours.

FINISHING PROCESS.

Fustic, 33 lbs.
Boil one hour.

FINISHING PROCESS.

Fustic, 33 lbs.
Supertartrate of potash, $2\frac{1}{2}$ lbs.
Boil two hours.

PREPARATION PROCESS.

Potash-sulphate of alumina, 5 lbs.
Murio-sulphate of tin, $2\frac{1}{2}$ lbs.
Boil one hour.

AGGREGATE PROCESS.

Fustic, 33 lbs.
Supertartrate of potash, $2\frac{1}{2}$ lbs.
Potash-sulphate of alumina, 5 lbs.
Murio-sulphate of tin, $2\frac{1}{2}$ lbs.
Boil one hour.

SULPHUR.

Quercitron bark, $2\frac{1}{2}$ lbs.
Potash-sulphate of alumina, $2\frac{1}{2}$ lbs.
Supertartrate of potash, 5 lbs.
Sulpho-muriate of tin, $2\frac{1}{2}$ lbs.
Use all these together, with the addition
of a very little of sulphate of indigo,

merely to give the peculiar tinge of the green due to the color of sulphur. Boil the wool one hour.

WELD YELLOW.

Weld, 100 lbs.
Potash-sulphate of alumina, 14 lbs.
Supertartrate of potash, 2 lbs.
Murio-sulphate of tin, 5 lbs.
Boil out the weld first, and withdraw the bag or bags; then add the mordant, and when that is dissolved, enter the wool, and boil one hour

WELD GOLD-COLOR.

Weld, or Woald, 100 lbs.
Potash-sulphate of alumina, 7 lbs.
Supertartrate of potash, 3 lbs.
Murio-sulphate of tin, 7 lbs.
Use these all together, and boil the wool up 'in them for three-fourths of an hour; then raise the wool out, and give from four to eight ounces (according to

shade) of grained cochineal, and boil one-half or three-fourths of an hour.

RECIPES FOR RED.

In dyeing the whole of this order of colors, much of the effect depends upon cleanliness, and taking care to have all the solutions clear and limpid, the alum, etc., as well as the rest of the dyestuffs, of a good quality, and free from any dirt or mixture of other materials. After dyeing, let them be washed off, and dried in the open air, with the exception of the woad colors, which are better if dried in the shade.

ROSE.

Nitro-muriate of tin, $4\frac{1}{2}$ pts.
Potash-sulphate of alumina, $4\frac{1}{2}$ lbs.
Supertartrate of potash, $4\frac{1}{2}$ lbs.
Cochineal, 6 lbs.
Boil the wool one half-hour.

CRIMSON.

Nitro-muriate of tin, 6 pts.
Potash-sulphate of alumina, 6 lbs.

Supertartrate of potash, 6 lbs.

Cochineal, 10 lbs.

Treat this color the same as the rose.

PINK.

Nitro-muriate of tin, 3 pints.

Potash-sulphate of alumina, 3 lbs.

Supertartrate of potash, 3 lbs.

Cochineal, 3 lbs.

When these articles are all thoroughly dissolved, enter the wool, and boil an hour or an hour and a half, and let it be washed off the same day; which course adopt with all colors having a mordant composed as the above. You will also make a paste of the cochineal, for all those colors which have the pink or crimson hue to them. The cochineal you will digest with equal weight of aqua ammonia, for twenty-four hours, [or longer, before using.

LAC SCARLET.

Young-fustic, 7½ lbs.

Best lac dye, 15 to 20 lbs.

Supertartrate of potash, 10 to 12½ lbs.

Nitro-muriate of tin, 10 to 12½ pts.

Boil one to one and a half hours; wash off all the scarlet colors, as soon as possible after coming from the kettle.

BUFF.

Supertartrate of potash, 5 lbs.

Quercitron bark, 1 lb.

Munjeet, 4 ozs.

Nitro-muriate of tin, 5 lbs.

SALMON, OR FLESH-COLOR.

Supertartrate of potash, 3 lbs.

Murio-sulphate of tin, 5 lbs.

Young-fustic, 2 lbs.

Lac-dye, ¾ lbs.

MELON.

Quercitron bark, 2½ lbs.

Munjeet, 3½ ozs.

Supertartrate of potash, 1½ lbs.

3

Potash-sulphate of alumina, 3 lbs.
Nitro-muriate of tin, 2½ lbs.

ORANGE.

Potash-sulphate of alumina, 5 lbs.
Supertartrate of potash, 2½ lbs.
Muriate of tin, 5 pts.
Quercitron bark, 33 lbs.
Munjeet, 2½ lbs.

AURORA.

Quercitron bark, 20 lbs.
Lac-dye, 8 lbs.
Supertartrate of potash, 8 lbs.
Murio-sulphate of tin, 8 lbs.
Potash-sulphate of alumina, 2 lbs.

FLAME-COLOR, OR SCARLET BARRE.

Young-fustic, 15 lbs.
Lac-dye, 12 lbs.
Supertartrate of potash, 10 lbs.
Murio-sulphate of tin, 1½ lbs.

MOCK SCARLET.

Best crop madder, 15 lbs.
Lac-dye, 7 lbs.

Supertartrate of potash, 8 lbs.

Nitro-muriate of tin, 10 lbs.

All of these colors are dyed with one hour's boil; then to be thrown out of the kettle, and thoroughly washed as soon as convenient.

LILAC.

MORDANT PROCESS.

Potash-sulphate of alumina, 5 lbs.

Supertartrate of potash, 1¼ lbs.

Boil two hours.

DYEING PROCESS.

Hypernic-wood, 5 lbs.

Logwood, 5 lbs.

Urine, 2½ galls.

Boil one hour.

LAVENDER.

MORDANT PROCESS.

Potash-sulphate of alumina, 7 lbs.

Supertartrate of potash, 2 lbs.

Bichromate of potash, 1 lb.

Boil two hours.

DYEING PROCESS.

Logwood, 8 lbs.

Urine, 2½ galls.

Boil one hour.

COMMON PURPLE.

Potash-sulphate of alumina, 12½ lbs.

Supertartrate of potash, 3 lbs.

Boil two hours. Leave the wool in all night; next day, wash.

DYEING PROCESS.

Hypernic-wood, 16 lbs.

Logwood, chipped, 16 lbs.

Urine, 3 galls.

Boil one hour.

COMMON WINE-COLOR.

MORDANT PROCESS.

Potash-sulphate of alumina, 12½ lbs.

Supertartrate of potash, 3½ lbs.

Boil two hours. Leave the wool in all night; next day, wash off.

DYEING PROCESS.

Hypernic-wood, 30 lbs.

Logwood, 10 lbs.

Urine, 2 qts.

Boil one hour.

CHROME–PURPLE.

Potash-sulphate of alumina, 10 lbs.

Supertartrate of potash, 3 lbs.

Bichromate of potash, 2 lbs.

DYEING PROCESS.

Logwood, 56 lbs.

Muriate of tin, 3 lbs.

Boil one hour.

CHROME–GREEN.

MORDANT PROCESS.

Bichromate of potash, 1½ lbs.

Supertartrate of potash 1 lb.

Potash-sulphate alumina, 1 lb.

Boil one hour, and let the wool remain all night.

DYEING PROCESS.

Logwood chips, 10 lbs.

Fustic chips, 20 lbs.

Urine, 1 gall. Boil one hour.

RIFLE GREEN.

MORDANT PROCESS.

Bichromate of potash, $1\frac{1}{4}$ lbs.

Supertartrate of potash, $1\frac{1}{4}$ lbs.

Potash-sulphate of alumina, $1\frac{1}{4}$ lbs.

Boil two hours.

DYEING PROCESS.

Logwood chips, $12\frac{1}{2}$ lbs.

Fustic chips, 12　lbs.

Sulphate of copper, 1 lb.

Boil one hour.

COMMON LOGWOOD GREEN.

Bisulphate of copper, 5 to $7\frac{1}{2}$ lbs.

Boil two hours.

DYEING PROCESS.

Logwood, 20 lbs.

Fustic, 25 lbs.

Work the wool in this for about half
an hour, at about one hundred and eighty
or one hundred and ninety degrees; then
give three pails urine, and work well for
another half-hour.

COSSACK GREEN.

Bichromate of potash, $1\frac{1}{2}$ lbs.
Potash-sulphate of alumina, 1 lb.
Supertartrate of potash, 1 lb.
Boil two hours.

DYEING PROCESS.

Fustic, 40 lbs.
Crop madder, 5 lbs.
Logwood, 7 lbs.
Sulphate of copper, 1 lb.
Boil one hour.
This green may be made perfectly fast by a very slight woading.

SADDENED COLORS.

All the information that can be given respecting dyeing these shades amounts to mere generalities; one of which is, to be certain to begin coloring with little enough dyestuffs, for more can be given if wanted; but if the quantity required by the pattern be exceeded, it will be difficult to work it off again. If it happen not to be brought up to the pattern by the first quantity of materials, give it more, and of such sorts, as, by a comparison of the pattern, you ascertain to be needed. If it requires to be made redder, only camwood must be given; if redder and bluer, cudbear, and perhaps a little logwood, or a trifle more saddening may be used. If it be short of yellow, give it fustic; but remember, always to leave them a little under the pattern in this respect, as the yellow always rises in a fawn or drab; and the red does some also, especially camwood. Always leave them finished a little on the saddening side of the pattern.

If they are not blue enough, give a little logwood, or sulphate of iron, according to your own judgment; if not green enough, perhaps a little sumach will give it that hue, or sumach and sulphate of iron together.

But, as before said, experience and judgment in the dyer are what is essentially necessary to the production of any pattern.

These kinds of colors may mostly be dyed either by using all the dyestuffs and the saddening together, or by first boiling on the dyestuffs, and then saddening afterwards.

PURE FAWN.

Crop madder, 2 lbs.
Camwood, 2 lbs.
Fustic, 2½ lbs.
Boil one hour and a half; then sadden with half a pound of sulphate of iron, and one half-hour's boil.

SANDY FAWN.

Madder, 2 lbs.
Camwood, 2 lbs.
Fustic, 2 lbs.
Boil one hour and a half; then sadden with eight ounces sulphate of iron and two ounces potash-sulphate of alumina, and half an hour's boil.

CHOCOLATE.

Cudbear, 3 lbs.
Camwood, 1 lb.
Fustic, 3 lbs.
Logwood, 4 ozs.
Boil one and a half hours; then sadden

3*

with three-fourths of a pound sulphate of iron, and boil half an hour's boil.

HARE–BACK.

Fustic, 3 lbs.
Camwood, 1 lb.
Madder, 6 lbs.
Boil one and a half hours; then sadden with three-fourths of a pound sulphate of iron, and three-fourths of a pound sulphate of copper, and half an hour's boil.

MULE-COLOR.

Crop madder, 1 lb.
Camwood, 1 lb.
Nutgalls, 2 lbs.
Boil one and a quarter hours; then sadden with three-fourths of a pound sulphate of iron, and half an hour's boil.

SLATE.

Logwood, 8 lbs.
Sumach, 2 lbs.
Fustic, 2 lbs.
Madder, 2 lbs.
Boil one and a half hours; then sadden

with two pounds sulphate of iron, and half an hour's boil.

DRAB SLATE.

Logwood, 16 lbs.

Camwood, 2 lbs.

Boil one and a half hours; then sadden with four pounds sulphate of iron, and three-fourths of an hour's boil.

This color to mix with puce, for slate mixture.

DRAB.

Fustic, $1\frac{1}{2}$ lbs.

Madder, $1\frac{1}{2}$ lbs.

Logwood, $\frac{3}{4}$ lb.

Sumach, $\frac{3}{4}$ lb.

Boil one and a half hours; then sadden with three ounces of potash-sulphate of alumina, six ounces sulphate of iron; half an hour's boil.

SILVER DRAB.

Fustic, 14 ozs.

Madder, 4 ozs.

Supertartrate of potash, 1 lb.

Sulphate of iron, $\frac{1}{2}$ oz.

Boil one and a half hours.

STONE DRAB.

Logwood 4 ozs.

Fustic, 2 lbs.

CLARET.

DYEING PROCESS.

Camwood, 65 lbs.

Logwood, 10 lbs.

Boil two hours.

MORDANT PROCESS.

Sulphate of copper, 5 lbs.

Sulphate of iron, 1 lb.

Boil one hour.

MULBERRY.

Woad to a middle blue, then wash off well.

DYEING PROCESS.

Camwood, 30 lbs.

Hypernic, 10 lbs.

Logwood, 5 lbs.

Boil two hours.

MORDANT PROCESS.

Sulphate of copper, 5 lbs.

Sulphate of iron, $\frac{3}{4}$ lb.

Boil one hour.

CORBEAU.

Camwood, 25 lbs.

Logwood, 25 lbs.

Fustic, 2½ lbs.

Boil one hour.

MORDANT PROCESS.

Sulphate of iron, 5 lbs.

Sulphate of copper, 1 lb.

BROWN OLIVE.

DYEING PROCESS.

Fustic, 50 lbs.

Crop-madder, 12½ lbs.

Logwood, 7 lbs.

Boil two hours.

MORDANT PROCESS.

Sulphate of iron, 2½ lbs.

Boil one hour.

CHROME–BLACK, ON TWELVE PIECES.

MORDANT PROCESS.

Six pounds chrome.

Three pounds tartar.

Boil one and one-half or two hours.

DYEING PROCESS.

One hundred and twenty-five or one hundred and fifty pounds logwood.

Three pails camwood.

Boil two hours, till shade is up. Leave these quite blue; they will darken in finishing.

COPPERAS-BLACK, FOR TEN PIECES DOESKIN.

MORDANT PROCESS.

Copperas, 18 lbs.

Blue vitriol, 6 lbs.

Tartar, 5 lbs.

Sumach, 10 lbs.

Bolted logwood, 25 lbs.

Put these all in together, and boil ten minutes; then add a little cold water. Enter cloths, and run one hour and a half with a gentle boil; then take them out, fold, and let them drain until the next day; and finish with —

Logwood, 15 lbs.

Camwood, 15 lbs.

Boil two hours.

TABLE OF MIXTURES.

BLUE MIXTURE,	{	20 White,
		80 Blue.
BLUE MIXTURE,	{	30 Puce,
		70 Mad. Blue.
IRON MIXTURE,	{	33 Light Blue,
		67 Black.
OLIVE MIXTURE,	{	20 Lemon Yellow,
		91 Black.
OLIVE MIXTURE,	{	20 Lemon Yellow,
		80 Black.
CLARET MIXTURE,	{	30 Bright Green,
		70 Claret.
VIOLET MIXTURE,	{	15 Yellow,
		85 Blue Violet.
VIOLET MIXTURE,	{	80 White,
		20 Blue Violet.
RHODODENDRON,	{	50 Full Puce,
		50 Olive.
HARE–BACK,	{	58 Drab,
		10 Red,
		5 Black.
PURPLE MIXTURE,	{	33 Crimson,
		67 Blue.

MULE MIXTURE, $\begin{cases} 30 \text{ Drab,} \\ 70 \text{ Blue Black.} \end{cases}$

PLUM MIXTURE, $\begin{cases} 30 \text{ Full Puce,} \\ 70 \text{ Dark Slate.} \end{cases}$

OXFORD MIXTURE, $\begin{cases} \frac{1}{4} \text{ White.} \\ 99\frac{3}{4} \text{ Rich Black.} \end{cases}$

FIRST BLACK MIXTURE, $\begin{cases} 2\frac{1}{2} \text{ White,} \\ 97\frac{1}{2} \text{ Black.} \end{cases}$

THIRD BLACK MIXTURE, $\begin{cases} 15 \text{ Puce,} \\ 85 \text{ Black.} \end{cases}$

STEEL MIXTURE, $\begin{cases} 15 \text{ to } 30 \text{ White,} \\ 85 \text{ to } 70 \text{ Black.} \end{cases}$

GREEN MIXTURE, $\begin{cases} 70 \text{ Middle Green,} \\ 30 \text{ Fast Lilac.} \end{cases}$

IRIS MIXTURE, $\begin{cases} 20 \text{ Yellow,} \\ 30 \text{ Red,} \\ 50 \text{ Blue.} \end{cases}$

SECOND
BLACK MIXTURE, $\begin{cases} 10 \text{ White,} \\ 90 \text{ Black.} \end{cases}$

SILVER–GRAY, $\begin{cases} 36 \text{ Slate, Light,} \\ 36 \text{ Purple,} \\ 28 \text{ White.} \end{cases}$

CADET MIXTURE, $\begin{cases} 33 \text{ White,} \\ 34 \text{ Black,} \\ 33 \text{ Blue.} \end{cases}$

PICKING-ROOM.

The wool, after being thoroughly dried, is carried to the picking-room, and run through the pickers. Then it is all laid on the floor, in a bed or pile, and oiled.

There are various qualities of oil used, according to the kind and style of goods you design to make. If you design to make a fine broadcloth or doeskin, you should, to each one hundred pounds of wool, put on one gallon of olive-oil, stirring it till the wool has absorbed the oil. Then give it two run through the picker, making three times that it has gone through. If it is now well open and light, it will do to go to the card; if not, it should be put through again.

Observe that you do not place the fluted rollers so near as to break the fibre, and reduce the wool thereby so as to destroy the staple.

The latest improved and best picker in use is manufactured by J. G. Sargent, Lowell, Mass. It is made with fluted rollers in front, to receive the wool from the apron. The main cylinder makes twelve hundred revolutions per minute, and is capable, if run at fifteen hundred, to pick four thousand pounds per day, if properly tended, and kept in good running order. The dirt and waste should be removed as often as the lots are changed. The picker-teeth should be carefully examined twice each day, to prevent them from flying out. In preparing mixtures, each lot should be picked separate the first time, and not mixed till oiled. After it is oiled, it should be well poled, and mixed as evenly as possible, before it is put through the picker.

CARDING-ROOM.

Carding the oiled wool is the next process in the woollen manufacture. It serves to open up and separate the woolly fibres, rendering the wool more light and equable.

The card consists of a first breaker, second breaker, and finisher. The main card or cylinder on the first breaker should be covered with straight-toothed clothing, and ground to a needle-point, which is done by the vibration of the grinder when grinding. In putting on new clothing, great care should be exercised, and draw it tight, smooth, and even. The small nails should be put in very even, working by a line. The speed of the cylinder should not exceed one hundred and twenty revolutions per minute. The doffer and workers should make twenty revolutions per minute. The second breaker should make the same speed as the first breaker. The finisher doffer differs considerably from the doffers on the first and second breakers. Instead of having its surface completely covered with card-clothing, in a spiral form, it has merely a succession of oblong card-clothing rings, fixed on it at intervals parallel to the axis; so that the wool is detached from the doffer by the comb, and carried continually through rubber rollers, that vibrate, and form the roping as it passes through, and is wound on large spools.

Then it is taken away, and placed on the jack for spinning. To regulate the size of roping, you will weigh, and change the gear until you obtain the desired size.

ROPING–TABLE.

For two run yarn, have roping one run.
For four run yarn, have roping two run.
For six run yarn, have roping three run.
For eight run yarn, have roping four run.
If it is found necessary to spin a little finer or a little coarser, you can vary, and put the yarn to compare with sample or size that the style of goods call for.

REDUCING WOOL ON THE CARDS.

For reducing wool on the cards, cross your worker-belt, and run it reverse. This change is very desirable on face goods. It makes more fibres, which is an essential point to be gained in finishing. It will give one-third more lustre, and goods will handle two qualities finer when the wool is carded with the belt reversed. In preparing mixtures, if you use three hundred pounds white wool of the first quality, and wish to put in forty pounds of black or blue, select the fifth or sixth quality, which will card out clear, be free from specks, and save hours of work in the specking-room.

SPINNING-ROOM.

The wool comes into the spinning-room in roping, wound on spools, when it is placed on the frame and adjusted. The roping ends are then taken singly, and carried through between small iron rollers, and attached to the upright bobbin, which is revolved by small bands from a tin drum running the whole length of the jack. This drum is driven by a large belt attached to the main driving-pulley.

The carriage, or jack, on which are placed the upright bobbins, vary in number from two hundred and forty to three hundred spindles. Two hundred and forty is the common or ordinary size, and used generally by the American manufacturer.

The jack is placed on grooved iron wheels, that run on an oval track about three yards in length. When the jack is pushed into gear, it takes from two to ten inches of roping from the spools; and then, as the jack is slowly drawn out, it twists and converts the roping into yarn, when it is wound by turning the crank with the right hand, the left hand placing the yarn on the bobbin by guiding the follower. The twist is regulated by the twist-plate, giving as many holes of twist as you think the yarn requires, or to suit the style of goods. The present method of ascertaining the size and regulating the fineness is determined and counted in runs. Sixteen hundred yards make one run, and weighs one pound avoirdupois.

SPINNERS' TABLE.

RUNS.	GRAINS.	RUNS.	GRAINS.
1	$218\frac{3}{4}$	$8\frac{1}{4}$	$26\frac{17}{33}$
$1\frac{1}{4}$	175	$8\frac{1}{2}$	$25\frac{25}{34}$
$1\frac{1}{2}$	$145\frac{5}{6}$	$8\frac{3}{4}$	25
$1\frac{3}{4}$	125	9	$24\frac{1}{36}$
2	$109\frac{3}{8}$	$9\frac{1}{4}$	$23\frac{24}{37}$
$2\frac{1}{4}$	$97\frac{2}{9}$	$9\frac{1}{2}$	$23\frac{1}{38}$
$2\frac{1}{2}$	$87\frac{1}{2}$	$9\frac{3}{4}$	$22\frac{17}{39}$
$2\frac{3}{4}$	$79\frac{6}{11}$	10	$21\frac{25}{40}$
3	$72\frac{1}{12}$	$10\frac{1}{4}$	$21\frac{11}{41}$
$3\frac{1}{4}$	$67\frac{4}{13}$	$10\frac{1}{2}$	$20\frac{35}{42}$
$3\frac{1}{2}$	$62\frac{1}{2}$	$10\frac{3}{4}$	$20\frac{15}{43}$
$3\frac{3}{4}$	$58\frac{1}{3}$	11	$19\frac{39}{44}$
4	$54\frac{11}{16}$	$11\frac{1}{4}$	$19\frac{4}{19}$
$4\frac{1}{4}$	$51\frac{8}{17}$	$11\frac{1}{2}$	$19\frac{1}{46}$
$4\frac{1}{2}$	$48\frac{11}{18}$	$11\frac{3}{4}$	$18\frac{29}{47}$
$4\frac{3}{4}$	$46\frac{1}{19}$	12	$18\frac{11}{48}$
5	$43\frac{3}{4}$	$12\frac{1}{4}$	$17\frac{6}{8}$
$5\frac{1}{4}$	$41\frac{2}{3}$	$12\frac{1}{2}$	$17\frac{1}{2}$
$5\frac{1}{2}$	$39\frac{17}{22}$	$12\frac{3}{4}$	$17\frac{8}{51}$
$5\frac{3}{4}$	$38\frac{1}{23}$	13	$16\frac{49}{52}$
6	$36\frac{11}{24}$	$13\frac{1}{4}$	$16\frac{27}{56}$
$6\frac{1}{4}$	35	$13\frac{1}{2}$	$16\frac{11}{54}$
$6\frac{1}{2}$	$32\frac{17}{26}$	$13\frac{3}{4}$	$15\frac{10}{11}$
$6\frac{3}{4}$	$32\frac{11}{27}$	14	$15\frac{5}{8}$
7	$31\frac{1}{4}$	$14\frac{1}{4}$	$15\frac{29}{57}$
$7\frac{1}{4}$	$30\frac{5}{59}$	$14\frac{1}{2}$	$15\frac{5}{58}$
$7\frac{1}{2}$	$29\frac{1}{6}$	$14\frac{3}{4}$	$14\frac{42}{59}$
$7\frac{3}{4}$	$28\frac{7}{31}$	15	$14\frac{7}{12}$
8	$27\frac{11}{32}$		

With this table, you will use the ordinary yarn-beam for weighing. The beam can be obtained from Sumner Pratt, of Worcester, Mass.

When you wish to ascertain the size of yarn, take from the jack five bobbins; reel from each five yards, which makes twenty-five yards, which place on the beam. It will give and correspond with the table. To ascertain the size of yarn, where two twists are put together, — say one of four run and one of six run fine, — add them together, and divide by four, allowing one-third for take-up, namely, —

Example : — 4, 6 = 10.
$$\div 4)\overline{10}(2.50 \text{ runs.}$$
$$8$$
$$\overline{20}$$

This shows the yarn would be two-and-a-half run fine.

SPOOLING–ROOM.

The warp-bobbins are brought from the jack to the spooler, where they are run off onto spools, and put on the dresser-rack for dressing. If you wish to make a warp with twenty-four hundred threads, you will spool six spools, with forty thread on a spool; that will give twenty-four hundred threads in the warp.

The average length of cuts are thirty yards; we will say six cuts to the warp; that would require one hundred and eighty yards of yarn. This you will regulate on the spooler by putting on the one hundred and eighty yards.

Set the clock on the spooler for one hundred and eighty yards; put forty thread on each spool. That will give, as before, twenty-four hundred threads in the warp.

THE REED.

The reed is a very important article in weaving. It divides the warp-thread, and may also determine the fineness of the

4

cloth; but a coarse web may be made in a fine reed, and a fine web may be made in a coarse reed; consequently, it is really the number of warp-threads contained in a given space that determine the fineness of the cloth or web.

For example:—A six-hundred web can be made in a twelve-hundred reed by putting only one thread in the split; and a twenty-four hundred can be made in the same reed by putting four thread in the split; or an eighteen-hundred,' by putting three hundred in the split. However, the common practice is to put two thread in the split; and when speaking about the fineness of a web, it is always understood that two threads are in the split. But in other places, there are different scales or rules by which the fineness of the web is named.

To ascertain and rate the reed:—

Example:—$2400 \div 40 = 60 \div 3 = 20$.

Divide the number of threads by the width you wish to make the cloth in the loom, and that result by the number of threads you wish to put into a dent; that will give the number of reed.

Twenty dents to the inch, three threads in a dent, forty inches wide, and twenty-four hundred threads in the warp. The same principle of calculation will apply in all cases; changing alternately as you determine and decide on the number of threads in the warp, or width of the cloth, and number of threads you put into a dent.

CALCULATION OF WARPS.

To find the number of ends in a warp, ascertain the number of ends in one inch, by the given quantity of inches, that are to be the width of the warp; and the answer the number of ends required.

Example: — $40 \times 60 = 2400$ ends in the warp. To find the weight of warp in one yard, divide the number of threads by the size of the yarn. Example: — $2400 \div 6 = 400$.

That gives, in a warp of twenty-four hundred threads, six-run fine, four ounces of yarn to the yard.

CALCULATION OF FILLING.

To find the quantity of filling for one yard of cloth, multiply the picks in one inch by the width. That will give the number of yards of filling in length in one yard.

Example :—$40 \times 36 = 1440$ yards of yarn in one yard.

To find the weight of filling for one yard, multiply as above, and divide by the size of the yarn. Example :—$40 \times 36 = 1440 \div 4 = 3\frac{60}{100}$.

Multiplying the number of picks to the inch, by the width of the cloth in the loom, and dividing by the number of runs, gives three ounces and sixty-three one-hundredths to the yard.

You will determine on the number of harness, say eight; and divide the number of threads in the warp by eight. That will give the number of heddles to put on each harness.

Example :— $2400 \div 8 = 300$ heddles.

DRAWING-IN.

When the warp is dressed, it is ready for the drawer-in. The beam is then hung up with two ropes, or iron hoops, about two feet from the floor, and a sufficient length of yarn turned off, so as to allow the end of it to come down to the drawer-in, who sits on a stool, with the heddles before him, — two rods inserted into where the lease-cords are. These lease-cords are put into the warp at the dresser. The ends of the rods are then fixed together, and the warp spread out to its proper breadth. The hander-in takes thread by thread, and hands it to the drawer-in to take through the heddles with a hook; and the drawer-in takes the heddles in regular succession, according to the draught of the warp. When the warp is drawn into the heddles, it next requires to be put into the reed, which is done by the same person, who has a reed-hook for the purpose. He commences at the right-hand side of the warp, and takes out the number of threads from the heddles that are intended to go into one dent. This operation being done, the warp is ready to be put in the loom.

PLAIN CLOTH

Is made by causing every thread of the warp and filling to cross each other at right-angles and tack together alternately. This is done by drawing the warp into two leaves of heddles, with equal quantities on each leaf. But a plain warp is in general drawn on four leaves, to keep the heddles from being too crowded on their shafts; and the two fore leaves are fixed together as one, and the two back ones as another, and mounted in the loom as if they were just two leaves. The figures shown on the following diagram exhibit the draught of a plain warp with four leaves :—

DIAGRAM No. 1.

4		
2	6	R
3		
1	5	S

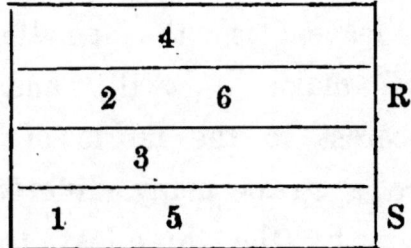

The figures 1, 2, 3, 4, 5, and 6, show
how the yarn is drawn through the heddles;
and R S are the shafts. They are sunk
and raised alternately, to form plain texture.
The term "plain cloth," as applied here,
must be understood as the kind of weaving;
as there are many fabrics made by plain
weaving that are not commonly called plain
cloth, but only to distinguish it from that
class of goods styled " fancies," which form
all the variety of twills and figures that
are made in the loom, by the warp and
weft being produced by the order and
succession in which the filling is interwoven
with the warp.

TWILLED PATTERN.

Three leaves is the smallest quantity that can make a twill, and its fabric comes nearest to the fabric of plain cloth. There are a great many different kinds of cloth made by the three-leaf twill.

From Diagram No. 2, it will be seen that two-thirds of the warp is on one side of the cloth, and two-thirds of the filling upon the other. This is accomplished by sinking two leaves and raising one every pick.

DIAGRAM No. 2.

	●			3
●				2
●				1

DIAGRAM No. 3.

3	6	1	4
2	5	2	5
1	4	3	6

It will also be observed that the yarn is drawn through the heddles as follows:— One thread on the first or front leaf, one thread on the second leaf, and one on the third or back leaf. The first harness is to

sink the first and second leaves, and raise
the third. The second harness is to sink
the first and third leaves, and raise the
second. The third harness is to sink the
second and third, and raise the first, and
repeat. To make what is called a herring-
bone twill, with three leaves, the same
harness will do; but the draught will be
as follows:—

Suppose the cloth is for a diagonal, and
the pattern twelve of brown, and twelve
of steel mixture; then the warp will require
to be drawn, as shown in Diagram 3, which
is six threads of brown drawn through the
heddles, beginning with the first leaf, and
six threads beginning with the third; the
steel-mixed is drawn in the same manner.
It will be observed that the twill turns
upon two threads, which does not make the
herring-bone so neat; but if it be drawn
as shown in Diagram 4, with ten threads

DIAGRAM No. 4.

3	6	9		13	16	19	
2	5	7	10	12	15	17	20
1	4		8	11	14		18

of brown, and ten of steel mixture, then the
twill will turn on one thread, which is the
proper way.

FOUR–LEAF PATTERN

Can be drawn straight over, as shown in

DIAGRAM No. 5.

		●		4	D	4 fourth.
	●	·		3	C	3 third.
●				2	B	2 second.
●				1	A	1 first.

The first shed is the back harness up,
and the other three down; the second is
the third harness up, and the other three
down; the third, is the second up, and
the other three down; the fourth, is the
first harness up, and the other down. This
is a simple pattern in weaving, or will be
considered so by an old weaver; but, let
the scholar understand this diagram thoroughly, and there will be no further diffi-
culty with other patterns. The first part
of the diagram is a representation of design paper; and the dark squares are the

warp threads, that are above the filling; and the white squares are those that are below it. The spaces that are marked A, B, C, and D, represent the harnesses; the figures 1, 2, 3, and 4, are the draught in the harnesses once over.

A FIVE–HARNESS PATTERN.

Diagram 6 is a regular five-harness pattern; and figure seven is what is called broken twill; and in these two diagrams

DIAGRAM No. 6.

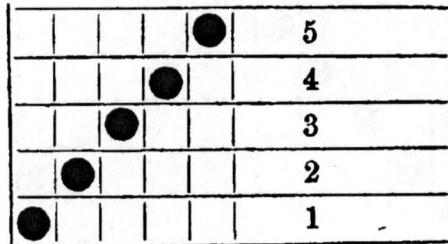

DIAGRAM No. 7.

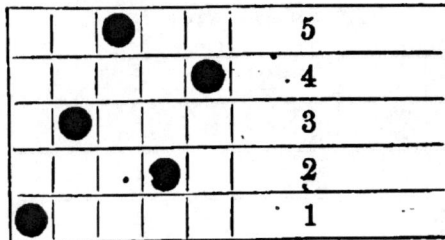

as in the other plans that follow, the

black squares are the leaves that are raised; and the white ones those that are sunk. On the pattern-chain they are styled sinkers and risers. Some designers call them offs and ons. The numbers 1, 2, 3, 4, and 5, are the draughts.

SIX–HARNESS PATTERN,

Diagram 8, is six-harness twill, and Diagram 9 is the same, broken.

DIAGRAM No. 8.

					●	6
				●		5
			●			4
		●				3
	●					2
●						1

DIAGRAM No. 9.

				●		6
		●				5
			●			4
	●					3
		●				2
●						1

DIAGRAM No. 10.

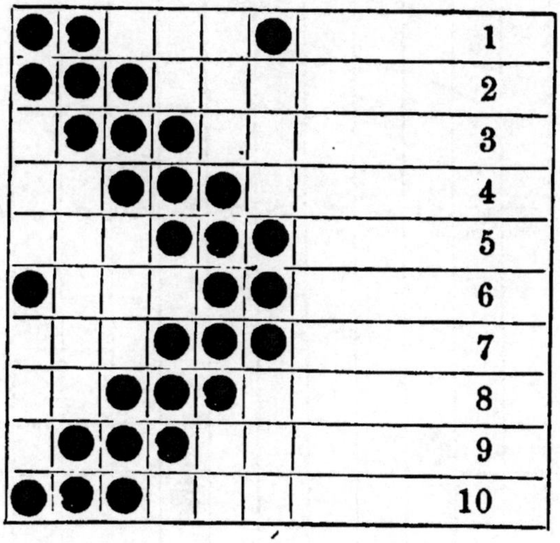

●	●				●	1
●	●	●				2
	●	●	●			3
		●	●	●		4
			●	●	●	5
●				●	●	6
			●	●	●	7
		●	●	●		8
	●	●	●			9
●	●	●				10

DIAGRAM No. 11.

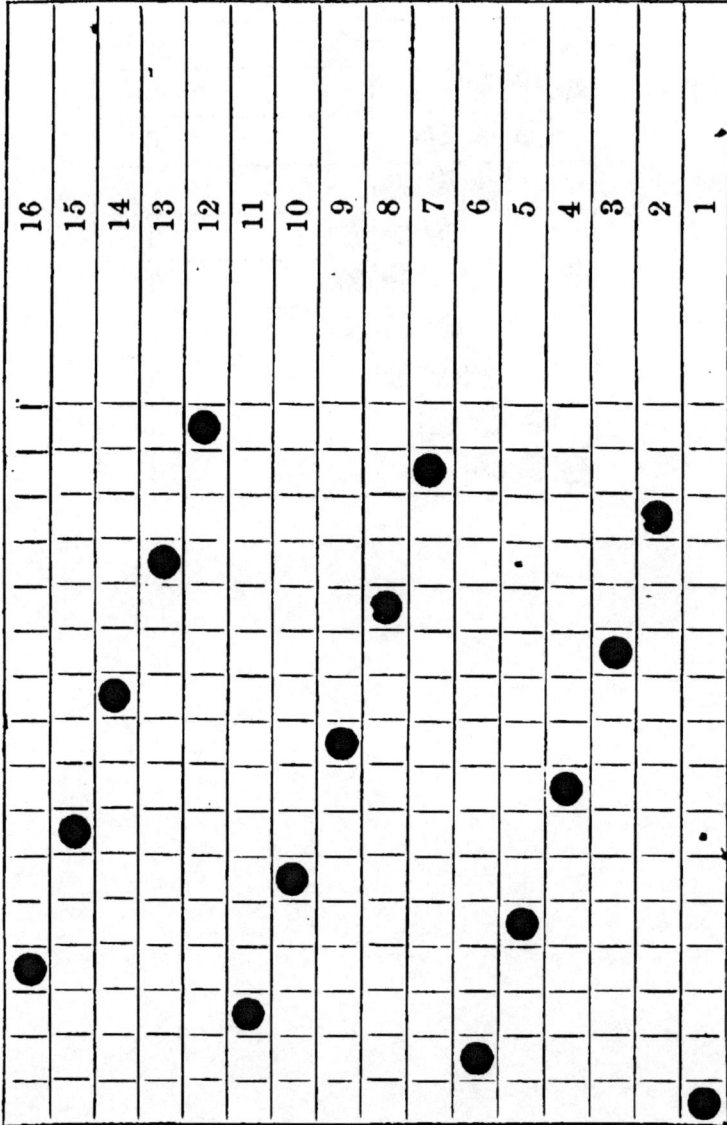

DIAGRAM No. 12.

●					●	●	●			1
	●				●	●				2
		●	●	●	●					3
		●	●	●						4
		●	●				●			5
●	●	●				●	●			6
●	●				●	●				7
●				●	●	●				8
●	●				●	●	●			9
●	●	●				●	●			10
		●	●				●			11
		●	●	●						12
		●	●	●	●					13
	●				●	●				14

Diagram 11 is called the full satin twill, and is an elegant pattern. With different twists and colors of yarn, it looks very nicely, especially with twists.

Diagram 12 is fourteen-harness pattern; is a sort of double figure, and looks very neat in fine cloth. With different mounting, you can obtain most any pattern desired.

DIAGRAM No. 13.

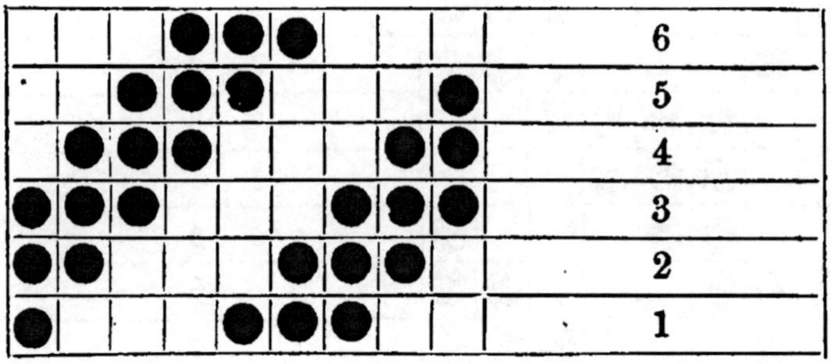

This pattern is wove with fourteen hundred and thirty-five threads in the warp. The reed has ten dents to the inch, four threads in a dent, five run warp.

The filling, two single drab threads, six run fine; and one double-and-twist, brown and white, three run fine, with forty-four picks to the inch; six harnesses, two hundred and forty heddles on each harness.

DIAGRAM No. 14.

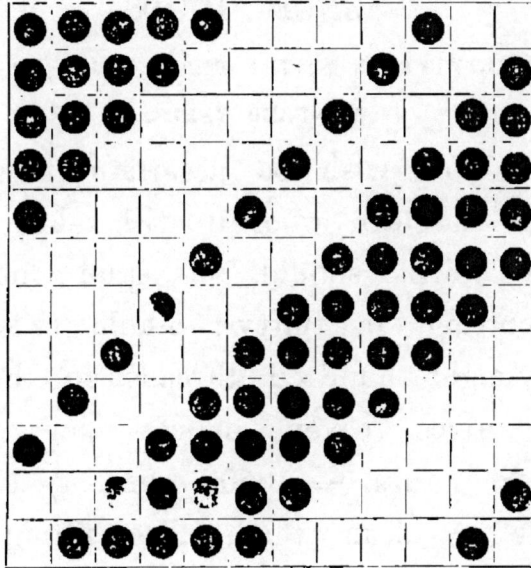

Fancy double-and-twist can be wove with single yarn, but will not be quite as heavy and strong as with double-and-twist.

The diagrams and examples · given will be sufficient to satisfy any ordinary mind on the theory of weaving; and, with two years' practice under a competent manufacturer, the art will be thoroughly understood.

DESIGN FOR FIFTY PIECES TWELVE-OUNCE GOODS:

SAY THIRTY YARDS TO THE PIECE, EQUAL TO FIFTEEN HUNDRED YARDS.

Now you wish to ascertain how many pounds of clean wool it will take.

The warp should be spun four runs fine, putting in thirty-two-hole twist, with twenty-eight hundred threads in the warp, which gives seven ounces per yard, — 1500 × 7 ozs. = 10500 ozs. ÷ 16 = 656 pounds of clean wool. The filling should be spun three and a half runs fine, and slay the warp thirty-six inches wide, putting in fifty picks to the inch, namely: — 50 × 36 = 1800 ÷ 3½ = 5 ozs., 1500 yards × 5 ozs. = 7500 ÷ 16 = 469 pounds of wool.

Which shows, to make fifteen hundred yards twelve-ounce goods, it will take four hundred and sixty-nine pounds of wool for the filling, and six hundred and fifty-six pounds for the warp.

To ascertain the number of reed, divide the number of threads, twenty-eight hun-

dred, by the width of cloth, 36 inch =
77, and that by the number of threads in
split, say four, that will give nineteen dents,
being the number of reed.

PRICE LIST.

PAID FOR PERFECT WEAVING BY THE PICK.

PICKS.	PRICE.	PICKS.	PRICE.
	c.		c.
12	1	54	4^2
18	1^2	57	4^3
21	1^3	60	5
24	2	63	5^1
27	2^1	66	5^2
30	2^2	69	5^3
33	2^3	72	6
36	3	75	6^1
39	3^1	78	6^2
42	3^2	81	6^3
45	3^3	84	7
48	4	87	7^1
51	4^1	90	7^2

One half-cent extra for pick and pick. Imperfect work will be charged according to damage.

BURLING-ROOM.

The cloth taken from the loom is brought to the burling-room, and measured; each piece is numbered, in succession, as it comes along. The number, yards, quality, and weight are taken, and entered in the books designed to receive the numbers, weights, etc., of the flannels. It is also marked on the cloth by the numberer, using a chain-stitch. This number remains on the cloth till finished, when it is taken off, and put on the ticket. In some mills, experts are employed to do this numbering and marking, who put on rare designs with silk, which remain on the cloth, and go to market, serving the purpose of a trade-mark. After numbering, it is then drawn over the burling-table, and all the small knots and threads, skip-ups, and uneven places taken off; all the holes are nicely darned with yarn the same color. If there are any mispicks, they are carefully drawn in, by a person who understands the pattern, thereby saving one-fourth of a yard, which would have to be allowed for a mispick. It would make an imperfect place in the cloth if not drawn in. When burled on both sides, it is drawn over the perch, and inspected by the Overseer. It is then carried to the

SCOURING AND FULLING ROOM.

The scouring and fulling are a very important part in making woollen cloth. The application of soap can be attended with so many different results, that it requires the most careful and strict attention on the part of the workman, as well as on the part of the proprietor, who should see that the best of material is used, in preparing the preparation for wetting-up in the scouring-mill, and soap for fulling.

If the alkali predominates in the soap, it will knock down all strong colors, more or less; and delicate colors it will entirely destroy, leaving them a mere shadow of what they would have been, if the proper strength of soap had been used. If the soap is too weak, and does not start the grease, the cloth will become cold; the soap will seem to lose its life; the longer it runs, till the cloth sets; when it will take a much stronger soap to start the grease, than it would if the right strength of soap had been applied first. If the soap is put on hot, the effect would be the same as if put on too strong. It will certainly start the color.

There are but few soapmakers who make it a study to get the right kind of stock, and have it properly made. I trust it will not be presuming, if I name one of the few who is acknowledged to be the best soapmaker in the United States, Emanuel Nathans, No. 1057, Tremont Street, Boston. Mr. Nathans is now furnishing some of the largest woollen mills, where the most delicate colors are made, and they all join in saying that this is the only soap they can use.

When the cloth has been scoured and dried, it is put into the fulling mill, saturated with soap; then the mill is started and run. If the cloth is light and slazy, it should be left thirty inches wide; but, if heavy and strong, it should be fulled up to twenty-eight inches wide. It should then be taken out, and put into the washer, and the soap thoroughly rinsed out.

When clean, fold them smooth, and lay on the scray to drain, ready for the

GIG–ROOM,

Which is another branch of the finishing, where the cloth receives the work and foundation for the beautiful polish to be found on all well-finished goods. If cloths are slighted and pushed along in the process of gigging, the effect is so certain and prominent, that it will not require an expert to see at once where and why the cloth looks so dull and lifeless when finished.

The gigging process consists of a continual teaseling of the cloth, by running it over large cylinders, in which are placed iron slats. Inserted in these slats are the teasel, a small burr, much like and resembling the common American bull-thistle. Many attempts have been made to substitute some metallic form for the teasel; but as yet, the effort has proved fruitless,—nothing has been found to take the place of this simple little burr.

The cloth is run till a heavy thick and is produced on the face of the goods, when it is taken and sheared or first cropped. Again it is taken back to the gig, and put through the process of second rising; sharper work is given to it, and run till it feels soft and pliable. It is then pressed and rolled; put in the steam box, and boiled for four hours; the water is then drawn off, the cloth put on the wet gig, and thoroughly washed with pure cold water. When done, it is steamed again.

This process is continued for three or four times; the number of times depends on the style of goods. When steamed they are ready for piece-dyeing. This kind of gigging will answer only for certain styles of goods. Fancy colors require different treatment in all the various processes of finishing.

SHEARING OR FINISHING ROOM.

The shearing machine is the most complicated, and requires more attention to keep it in good working order than any machine in the woollen mill; but when it does work well, there is no machinery process that its work shows at once, and gives the satisfaction as the shear.

The first work to be done on the cloth, is, to crop, second crop, and then comes the finishing, which is done by running it through the shear five or six times, placing the blade on the set screws. Then as you wish to shear a little closer, you will change the sets, running it through each time till you get a short, full face. Then it is taken by the speckers, and all the little specks and threads taken out. If the specks are numerous, and hard to pull out, it is better to ink them with a preparation prepared for the purpose, which is put on with a stick or quill.

They are then inspected over the perch, and all the holes are nicely fine-drawn;

when they cannot be drawn, a string is put in, to call attention when they are measured. After they have been inspected by the inspector, they are put on the brush and run for an hour, when they are taken and papered for the press.

Two days are consumed for pressing; when they are unpapered, and placed on the table, and measured, rolled, and packed, ready for market.

Lightning Source UK Ltd.
Milton Keynes UK
UKOW022018100912

198792UK00009B/89/P

9 781276 047913